Generational Farming

Keeping the Farm & the Family Together

By Pat Keating

This information is not a complete summary or statement of all available data necessary for making a financial decision and does not constitute a recommendation. Every situation is unique and you should consider your financial goals, risk tolerance and time horizon before making any financial decision. Please consult with your financial advisor about your individual situation. Any opinions are those of Pat Keating and not necessarily those of Raymond James. Expressions of opinion are as of this date and are subject to change without notice.

Changes in tax and other laws may occur at any time and could have a substantial impact upon each person's situation. While we are familiar with the provisions of the issues presented herein, as Financial Advisors of RJFS, we are not qualified to render advice on tax or legal matters. You should discuss tax or legal matters with the appropriate professional.

Susan Austin is not affiliated with Raymond James.

Here's What's Inside...

Introduction

June 2014
Manhattan, Kansas

One of the things my farmer clients tell me when they come to see me is "I'm tired of thinking about this". The "this" they are referring to, is how to keep the family farm in the family but be fair to all their children. They've seen firsthand the effects of what happens if this issue isn't resolved properly and want a solution that is fair to everyone while also minimizing the effects of taxes on their estate.

I've been working with clients just like this for the last 30 years and have seen what it looks like when it's handled well and everyone is happy. I've also seen the devastating effect not having a strategic plan in place has on families when farms have to be dismantled and sold under duress.

This book is a result of the exact process I have used with many families to clarify and bring closure to these concerns.

Following is an interview where I show you how to avoid having siblings who will no longer enjoy Thanksgiving Dinner together, and protect your interests so you can continue to live on the farm you've spent a lifetime working and maintain control for as long as you want.

I hope this book helps you determine the best way to keep your children on speaking terms, both the one who wants to stay on and farm and those who choose to pursue other careers.

Enjoy the book!

Pat Keating
Financial Advisor

Generational Farming!

Susan: Good afternoon, this is Susan Austin. With me today is Pat Keating from Manhattan, Kansas. Welcome Pat.

Pat: Hello, Susan; happy to be with you today.

Why Do Families Struggle to Keep the Farm and the Family Together?

Susan: We are going to talk about Keeping the Farm and the Family Together. Why are families *not* able to keep the farm and the family together Pat?

Pat: For many people, farming is not what they want to do. So even though they may have been born and raised on a farm, often not all of the children want to continue to farm. Maybe only one of them does. The rest of the children have chosen other professions which have led them in other directions.

Land values have gone up so much over the years now there's a tremendous amount of assets owned by the parents. Upon their death, those assets have to be divided because of family members who don't want their money tied up in the land. The problem becomes how to keep the farm together and keep the family still talking to each other.

Therefore, we have to have some way of creating liquidity that allows one child in the family to keep the farm and land, yet treats the other children in a fair manner according to the wishes of the parents.

Susan: What happens when this isn't handled before the parent's pass away?

Pat: Unfortunately, it's just a matter of time before the other family members decide they no longer want to have an investment in farmland. They may be receiving some rent income, but decide they need to sell the property so they can use the money for their own families to either purchase a home, send their children to college or maybe they have other business opportunities they want to pursue.

What potentially happens then is a forced liquidation or forced sale of the farm. Because the price of the land has continued to accelerate so much, the farming sibling may not be able to afford buying the brothers and sisters out. That's probably the biggest issue. But the biggest relationship issue comes once it's realized that even the sibling working the farm cannot stay there any longer when other family members want their equity position out of the land.

How Land Appreciation Is Costing Families Their Farms...

Susan: Are you seeing people having to break up and sell their farm just because they're not able to get the cash to buy the siblings out?

Pat: Absolutely. This is something that's been happening for many years. I started doing seminars and workshops on this in the early '80s talking about the issues of rising farm prices. This is not a new problem. It's a problem that's been going on in every family, in every rural community. Farmers see other families who are being totally destroyed and broken up because of this exact situation where the land had to be sold to divide up the assets of the parent's estate.

The problem certainly accelerated recently when land prices jumped dramatically throughout the Midwest. Because of these appreciated land values they're no longer able to buy out their siblings as hoped.

Susan: Right, if they thought they had a solution, as you point out, rising land values may have eliminated it because the land the farm is sitting on is now worth so much more. What kind of increases are we seeing in land value?

Pat: Land that sold a few years ago for maybe $1,000 an acre is now bringing anywhere from $5,000 to $10,000 an acre.

Susan: Quite an increase.

Pat: One thing about a family-owned farm which is different than owning a company or real estate or stock holdings is this is all about the land. It's not about the equipment. It's not about the livestock or the grain. It's about the land. Can they keep this land intact and continue to farm it as generations have before them?

For most people, when parents pass away it's always an emotional thing. Maybe their parents own a house. They might own a vacation home. They may own a stock portfolio. They have their own retirement plan and so forth. Those things don't have the same emotional tie however. Maybe the home you grew up in does, but most of the time these things don't cause emotional uproar.

However, when your ancestors were all farmers and you put this land in there that they've walked and played on as a child, it becomes a really tough, emotional issue to deal with.

Why They Are Tired of Thinking of a Solution...

Susan: When someone comes to see you to resolve this, what frame of mind are they in?

Pat: Most of the people who come in to me, are now 60 years of age or older. They've been thinking about this problem for many years. To be frank, they're tired of the concern about who is going to get the land and who isn't, and will certain children be upset because they didn't feel they were being treated fairly? They are tired of thinking about it.

People who come in say, "How are we going to resolve this problem so my one son or daughter can stay on the farm and farm it, and still treat the other children equally? What are we going to give them as their part of the inheritance?" If we give the farm to just one child, we have essentially disinherited the other children. But all of their money is tied up in the land, the improvements on the land, and the buildings on the land. So in effect there is no other source of funds to leave other children to compensate.

Most of these people do not have other liquid assets. They may have some equipment, livestock, and maybe some retirement money. But most all their money has been put back into the land.

Susan: They have all their eggs in the one basket, the land in this case. So it becomes, how can you divide the land up in a way that's fair to the other siblings who don't want to farm?

Pat: That's right because the other siblings, for whatever reasons, have no desire to stay on the farm. Or maybe the farm isn't big enough for everyone to make a living. Not everybody wants to be in that profession because farming is a way of life. It is not necessarily something people go into as a business to make a lot of money. They do it because it's a way of life. It's a part of their life. It's part of being on the land. It's part of being independent in that manner.

Susan: This can be a pretty emotional issue for folks, I imagine.

Pat: It's a very stressful issue. The parents may have inherited this land from their parents. Many of the people I talked to experienced this themselves - they experienced it 30 years ago in the '80s when their parents died, and the problems they had with their brothers or sisters when the land was divided then. Now, it's coming around again.

They may have had a very negative experience already once in their lifetime when their parents died, and the land was divided or sold. Many of the farmers we talk to have already been through this once in their own generation and they don't want their children to have to go through the same thing.

Susan: It's a shame rising land prices, which for a farmer should be a positive thing, could drive a wedge between some of these families. I can see the problem though, because if you aren't the one who is going to inherit the farm, you want your share, but there is no cash sitting around to make it equal.

Pat: In every community in rural America, that exact thing has happened where brothers and sisters no longer speak to each other, haven't spoken to each other for many, many years, and it was all over the argument and the fight when dad and mom died of how the property was divided. Every farm family out there knows a family like that. There is not one family that comes to my office that doesn't know specific cases of that exact thing happening and they do not want to see it happen in their own family.

Here Are 3 Mistakes to Avoid When Dividing up Your Estate...

Susan: Can we talk about some of the mistakes you've seen over the years when parents divide up the land?

Pat: One of the very first mistakes is they set up wills and trusts which gives an <u>undivided</u> interest to each of the children thinking that those children will all agree on what to do going forward. If there are five children, they give an undivided interest in the real estate of one-fifth interest to everybody. This creates a lot of problems. It creates a bigger problem if one of the siblings wants to sell.

I'm dealing with a situation right now where this exact thing happened. The farm was divided up into three different families which potentially further divides the land. Now, we have one family who wants to sell but the other families don't. Because of the law, they can force the land to be sold. That's probably the first and biggest mistake I see parents make when dividing up the land. Giving this undivided interest thinking their family members will get along in the future. Or thinking this is the fairest way to handle this issue.

Susan: When you say they give <u>undivided interest</u>, can you clarify what that means?

Pat: Sure. When you have a piece of real estate and remember, that's what we're talking about here. We're not talking about the equipment. We're not talking about the grains or cattle raised on the land.

It's always about the land. When you have a parcel of land, say 640 acres, it's all under one title, one legal description.

A mistake I often see is they give each of their children an undivided interest in the land which means you don't have any particular acreage you own. You just own part of all of it. That's where one of the problems comes in, because you have no way of saying, "Okay, we will take our portion of land and leave." When you have an undivided interest, then you have a problem because everybody has to stay together forever or until you do something else to resolve the problem.

One of the tools we use to resolve this is by using a limited liability company which is a separate entity, a corporate type of entity. By using these, we are able to set aside both voting and non-voting stock, which says who gets to vote and who doesn't. Then you can actually give away the non-voting stock interest of the LLC and leave the voting stock to the person you want to run the farm.

It doesn't solve the whole problem but it certainly solves the problem of being able to continue to run the farm business in the future. There's a lot of things going on at any time on a farm and you have to have someone making the decisions. That's one of the things we look at. Farm people do not use tools such as limited liability companies to the extent that they should.

Susan: Let me see if I understand you correctly. In a case where you have 640 acres, mom and dad thought they were being fair by giving each of their children an undivided interest in it. They think it's the fairest way to divide the land because then everyone has an equal share. But when some of the kids want out there's literally no way to handle the transaction because it's not cash that they can divide up and say, "here you go, here's your share."

Pat: Right. Something has to be sold and somebody has to buy. Another really important concern that is unfortunately part of our society today is the concern of divorces. Divorces of our children. How does that affect what happens to the land if we give it to them? They don't want their share of land being tied up in a divorce and now being forced to sell to solve a divorce decree, which I see all the time. Another issue we have to be careful of is what happens when we have children or grandchildren with special needs? Have we unintentionally disqualified them from government benefits?

These are all issues you must pay attention to when you get into the transfer of property. If you don't, then you've created problems in the future.

All of these issues are things people are tired of thinking about, and they want to know how they can solve them.

Susan: What are other mistakes you see when they try to solve this issue?

Pat: The 2nd and probably the biggest mistake is they do nothing. They simply ignore it. They hope that the problem will go away. Ignoring this is probably the worst thing they can do. When ignored it causes huge problems for the siblings and that's when things really break down and families break apart.

The 3rd mistake I see is not creating liquidity inside of the family's business to buy other members out. Liquidity is critical because for most farm people, they take all the money they make and either buy more land or buy more equipment. When most profits are reinvested there is no liquidity to fund siblings who don't want to farm.

If there is no money to buy someone out, then at some point there is a forced liquidation. It's the same pattern over and over again. Sometimes, they just ignore it. Sometimes, they make promises they can't keep. Sometimes, they've given this undivided interest which just delays the problem only to be addressed at some point in the future, when there is no cash to give other family members. These are the mistakes I see all the time.

What happens next is the family member working the farm may be forced to buy his brothers and sisters out at a very high price. To do that, they have to borrow the money with no control over current interest rates. They may not have enough leverage to be able to buy them out. For example, if there are five children in the family, and they've got to buy the other four out, obviously, they only have 20% of the equity position; therefore they do not have enough collateral to get the loan to buy out the other family members. No bank is going to loan 80% to someone who only owns 20%. These are big problems to have.

How Doing Nothing Can Lead to an Unwanted Auction of Your Farm...

Susan: What would someone do in that position, where if the four family members are saying, "We don't want the farm," but he doesn't have the money to buy them out, how are they supposed to resolve this?

Pat: They almost can't. What typically happens is the land goes up for auction. Someone else buys it, and the family farm has now been totally dissolved and the one the parents wanted to be able to stay and farm no longer is able to do that, and they move off the farm and find a job somewhere else.

Susan: That is a disaster.

Pat: It happens when this issue is not addressed properly before the parents pass away.

How to Keep Control of Your Farm...

Susan: You mentioned earlier that the parents want to be able to stay on the farm for their lifetime. How do they keep control while living but make sure everything goes the way they want when they pass?

Pat: You make a good point, because most farmers never retire. They want to spend their entire life on the farm. Sometimes because of health or whatever, they may not be able to, but they want to stay their entire life on that farm. My great grandfather bought a small parcel of land when he came here from Ireland. It went to my grandfather. My father was one of nine boys who were born and raised on the farm. He lived there his entire life and never moved away from it, and died in the house he was born in. He never wanted to leave. It's not unusual in that area.

They want to stay there for the rest of their lives. Because farmers are a very independent people, they want to take care of themselves, and they want to stay in control. They have no desire to give up control. How are we able to do that? If you create a limited liability company, using both voting and non-voting stock, then the parents could keep all the voting stock during their lifetime and give away some of the non-voting stock.

The advantage to that is it is very easy to transfer the farm out using the annual exemptions they have. They'd be able to give non-voting stock to whomever they want. They could have an agreement for a buy-sell between family members in the event of a parent's death. The other children would have to sell back the stock at a set price to the family member who wanted to stay on the farm. You preset the price, which means the parent has never given up the control.

We say they never retire. They may slow down. We have farm people who come in, in their '70s, and they're still out there working every day in their farm. They enjoy it. That's their passion. But that's how you keep them in control and you keep them there for their entire lifetime, if that's what they want.

How an LLC Can Help You Transfer the Land and Prevent Heartache...

Susan: Can I ask you a couple of clarifying questions? You mentioned an LLC, and voting and non-voting stocks earlier. Can you describe for us, in layman's terms, how those work?

Pat: A limited liability company (LLC) is simply a business entity; no different than any other corporation whether an "S" or "C" type. It's just taxed a little bit differently. The limited liability company is actually set up by the parents to begin with. They transfer the land inside it and the only thing the LLC owns is the land.

The parents own 100% of both voting and non-voting stock. You might have 10% voting and 90% non-voting. What they're able to do then over their lifetime, is gift away shares of stock instead of gifting away undivided interest in land. They gift away the non-voting shares. When they gift non-voting shares, they still have 100% control because they retain the voting stocks.

Then you're able to set up a buy/sell agreement. A buy/sell simply says at a named event someone buys and somebody sells. The parents then have a plan that says in the event of their death, certain children would sell their stock to the child who is going to stay on the farm for a set price. That price could be reviewed annually or whatever. Now, they know they're in control and they also know that the person working on the farm can stay.

When you do that, you could also enter into other types of agreements. One of them might be that the property's not going to be sold but will be leased or rented to the one child at a set price for a number of years.

Susan: The difference between voting stock and non-voting, is it two different types of shares?

Pat: One votes and one doesn't. It's like you can have all the stock you want but if you don't have the share that votes, you can't say anything about how the business is run, can you?

Susan: Interesting. The voting stock gives you control but the non-voting is ownership. Is that correct?

Pat: Yes, it is ownership. You could have a plan whereby the parents might eventually only own 10% at the time of their death. If we were trying to resolve an estate tax issue, we know as of today we have $5.2 million dollars of exemptions at death or $10.5 million for a family. But if the farm value has grown to more than that, now we have an estate tax issue. For amounts over $10,680,000, we have a very high estate tax issue.

By giving away stock every year it allows you to stay below that estate tax issue. But you didn't really give anything away because you only gave away the non-voting stock. So it solves two problems. The control stays with the parents and you avoid potential tax issues.

Susan: Interesting. If this isn't done properly and they pass away and their estate is worth $20 million because of the land value, it could entail a big tax bill that needs to be paid. Is that true?

Pat: The kids wouldn't inherit it but the estate would owe it. The estate would owe $3.6 million in taxes just for the estate tax alone. Remember, because we have the liquidity problem we mentioned earlier, this means you're forced to start selling off property to pay the estate taxes. But many times, it's not a tax issue; it's a transfer issue.

The tax issue can be solved. Many farm families estates aren't over ten million dollars. That's not the issue. It's the transfer problem that's the real problem.

Susan: Meaning how are you going to transfer this to your offspring in a fair way?

Pat: Yes, exactly.

Here's How to Get Your Legacy Plan Written so All Family Members Feel Valued...

Susan: Let's dive in then, what do you recommend they do Pat?

Pat: We sit down with the parents first. We spend time with them to get really clear on what their goals and objectives are. What is it they really want to have happen? What is their ideal wish list for this? Once we do that, we are clear on how to draft the plan from there.

Normally we start with just the parents. Then, contrary to what a lot of people think, I recommend they bring not only children into the discussion but their children's spouses as well. Because if there's an issue with the spouse of a child, I want to know it now, not later. The spouse is going to want to know what's going on as soon as that child comes home anyway. The spouse is going to ask, "What did you talk about?"

We have an open discussion so everybody hears the same thing at the same time. This meeting is one we run, so we're the moderator. We're not putting mom and dad in the awkward position of trying to run this meeting as well. That's when we cover all these issues and explain everything to everyone.

Susan: Is it generally handled in one meeting?

Pat: Yes, the family meeting is pretty much one meeting. Many farm families want to resolve this issue once and for all and they're thrilled there's a plan, and it's handled because they too have the same desires their parents have. They just want to make sure they're being treated fairly.

Specifically, one way you could treat everyone fairly is if you have liquidity. Liquidity can be created from several sources. Equipment can be sold off. The grains can be sold off. The livestock can be sold off. They may have a retirement plan. That generally isn't the issue anyway. As we stated earlier, the land is the issue.

A lot of farmers are reluctant to have significant amounts of life insurance to create the liquidity needed at the last parent's death to ensure enough cash to pay everybody else off. That contributes to the biggest issue because otherwise you have to borrow the money, and you never know what that cost is going to be or if that is even an option. Having the right amount of life insurance solves a lot of problems.

Susan: Right.

Pat: I remember when interest rates soared to 18%. Today, everyone thinks interest is always going to be 3% and 4%. Interest rates change and will certainly change again someday.

Susan: The siblings who want to invest in another direction or buy a house, even though the family wants to keep the farm together; it doesn't mean that the other siblings aren't going to want some sort of something...?

Pat: Cash. It's always cash.

Focus on Fair Not Equal...

Susan: I see. Walk me through how we make this right, so everyone is happy and the farm is kept in the family. What does it look like?

Pat: The first and probably most important thing is to let the parents understand they can write their own rule book. A rule book is just a set of instructions they create to dictate what should happen when they pass. The rule book could be their own revocable living trust. They can hold the land "in trust", which is a fancy way of saying, an agreement that the land will be held for the benefit of another party. By putting the land in a trust we eliminate probate, which is highly recommended. You don't want a third party dictating what happens to your family farm after you pass away. Mostly no one wins when that happens.

We work with the parents and set up the rules as to who is going to receive the land, whether they're going to get it outright, or whether they have the right to rent the property for a period of time. That's the first thing we address.

The second thing we have to address is how are we going to treat the other children? The first thing we always want to remove from people's vocabulary is the word "equal" because when you talk about treating everybody equal, it's absolutely impossible without a large amount of cash to divide. Without that you can never get to the word equal.

So we remove "equal" and use the word "fair." Getting them to understand what is fair and what isn't. The only people who get to determine what's fair by the way, are the parents. It's their money; it's their land. They make the decision.

Thanksgiving Dinner Is at Stake...

Susan: Interesting. I would imagine when they get this right, this changes everything. For farm families who don't address this, it can be devastating for their family. Everything they don't want to happen, which is breaking up the family and breaking up the farm, could be a result of not getting this handled correctly.

Pat: If you get it right, then you can tell the parents their land will be transferred to the next generation the way they want it to be, and their family will continue to be very close knit. And they can all sit down and have Thanksgivings together. If you get it wrong, the land they love and spent all of their life on will be sold and be broken up into multiple pieces, and the odds are high that some family members will never speak to each other again. The negative impact is huge, and no one wants to get it wrong.

Susan: Right. There's a lot at stake here.

Pat: There's a lot at stake here. This is different than other types of business ownership, investments, or anything else. This is a very high, emotional belief in a way of life and what you stand for. This is critical. The interesting thing about farm families is most of all the land and the properties owned carry the name of the family they bought the land from. That just tells you the respect people have in a farm community for the tradition of owning this land.

When someone buys someone else's land, as long as they own it, they will refer to the land by the name of the person they bought it from . It tells you how important it is for them to keep their own, as they call it, home place. It is so important to keep the land in place it makes the stakes very high in this planning process.

The Process Works Even if You've Employed the Services of a CPA and Lawyer...

Susan: What if they already have someone who helps them with their bookkeeping? Or maybe they have a CPA in the family, what happens then?

Pat: That's no problem. One of the things we do early on is identify all of the participants of the team. Those team members could be their accountant, their attorney, and/or their banker. The people we think we need to bring in should be brought in sooner rather than later. We're going to allow them to help identify the team members they want to have involved. If they have a trusted accountant or attorney they use, so be it. We're going to use their accountant or their attorney.

Now, if we do not believe the accountant or attorney is capable, we will tell them that as well; that we don't think that person has the expertise to help in this instance but we're going to let them bring together their team. We coordinate their team for them and try to use people they want to work with. Normally, a critical team member will be the bank. We have to make sure we have a good banking relationship because we don't know if we're going to need the banker tomorrow or 20 years from then. We need to make sure we're in tune with their banker.

How Your Legacy Plan Brings Confidence...

Susan: I would imagine there is a huge relief in getting this handled.

Pat: Yes, and the relief is a very exciting thing. You can see it in their faces. You can see it in their mannerism and they are just thrilled they now have a plan. A plan they understand and a plan they know they can change. They know once the death occurs, nobody else can change the plan because they set the rule book.

Susan: Right. It's funny that they'll have such relief when they're done with it but there is such resistance to get started...

Pat: The reason they're resistant to get started is because most of them have a very close family relationship now. They are very concerned that by having this discussion now, they might isolate some family members because they have seen too many times the problems other families had. As humans, we have a tendency to postpone things we think will create discomfort or stress.

Susan: It sounds like actually the opposite will happen.

Pat: That will happen but there is also a time when certain family members may become very upset when they realize they are not going to receive this property or they might not even receive an amount equal to the value of their share of the property because of the parents rules. Even though farm land may be selling for X amount per acre, they want the farming family member to get it for less. That's an issue you have to get through.

Susan: Very good, and you're saying to put it on the table for everyone so they know what the plan is. It doesn't become a family secret that way and turn into something bigger.

Pat: If it's put on the table while both parents are alive, the problem can be solved. It's very difficult to solve the problem once the parents are deceased.

Susan: I want to highlight you mentioning all cards are on the table with a third party mediator, which is important because emotions in families do tend to run high. If someone feels like they're not getting a fair deal, I would imagine it could go sideways pretty fast.

Pat: It absolutely can. Not only is a third party mediator important. It's extremely important everyone understands what's going on in that farm family, understands the agri world, the farm world, and understands the obstacles preventing this from being a successful plan.

Here's What Can Happen When You Get it Wrong...

Susan: Can you give an example of a scenario you've seen where it hasn't worked well?

Pat: I have a situation right now. My client owns a half interest in a parcel of land. In this particular case there are two other parties who each own a fourth. One of those parties died and gave their interest to a charity. The charity is now demanding the property to be sold so they can get their cash out. The land was probably worth $400,000 five years ago. Today, when I got the appraisal back, it's worth $780,000. The tenant wants to buy it. I'm probably going to offer it to the tenant for $850,000 and they'll probably buy it at that price.

In this case the other parties don't want to sell. But they have no choice. They don't have the $200,000 to give to the charity. That's what's going on in the real world and people are saying, "You know what? Hey, if I can get $200,000 from my fourth interest, give me the money. I'll take the cash." The charity says, "Forget about us being charitable. We want our $200,000." That's happening all the time here, and all over the country and will continue to do so because they don't make any more land.

Susan: I imagine it will. This has been very enlightening, Pat. I can see where a path which can keep the Farm in the family, give all the kids a fair share and a way to do it so they will still sit down and have Thanksgiving dinner together would be important. I really think this is valuable information as it can save a lot of heartache.

Pat: One of our main responsibilities is to show our clients all the tools that are available, how they work, and the advantages and disadvantages of each tool. It is the client's responsibility to decide which tool fits their situation. As you may imagine, you may not fully understand the LLC right now. You might not understand the revocable trust right now. You may not understand some of the lease agreements or how to put buy/sell agreements in place. It is our responsibility to explain the tools and how they work. Ultimately the decision becomes the client's on which tools they want to use and makes it their plan, not ours.

Here's How to Get Your Legacy Plan in Place...

Susan: Very well said. If someone wants to work on their plan to get this right, how do they get in touch with you, Pat?

Pat: Obviously, they can call us at 785-537-0366. Or, they can contact us through our internet site which is www.KeatingInc.com. Those are probably the two easiest ways to reach us, to help them through this process.

Susan: Very well said. Thank you.

Pat: Thank you.

Here's How to Keep the Family Farm in the Family...

You've been worrying about how to divide up the farm fairly to your children and grandchildren when you pass away. In fact, you're sick and tired of trying to come up with a way that everyone will be happy with. You worry this could damage the relationships you treasure most, as you've seen it happen to others in your community when they didn't have a plan in place that was fair to everyone, before they passed.

That's where we come in. We help people just like you structure a customized Legacy Plan to ensure you get to stay on the farm you've worked so hard on for so long, yet provide a fair and clear plan for your children and grandchildren.

Step 1: We spend 30 minutes together making sure we are a good fit for each other and flushing out your vision and fully addressing all of your concerns.

Step 2: We take you through a 60 minute process to share with you the strategies and options available to keep the family farm intact and allow whomever wants to stay on and farm, the ability to do so without incurring tremendous debt or taxes to pay off their siblings.

Step 3: We take it from here and design your Legacy plan. Our team of professionals does the due diligence required and crafts your individualized strategic legacy plan so that you can have the confidence for your family you've been craving.

Most people are unsure about the best approach to keep the family farm in the hands of the family member they want.

Now you can get your Legacy plan in place, keep the farm in the family, and sit down and enjoy Thanksgiving dinner the way it was meant to be...together.

If you'd like us to help, just call us at (785) 537-0366 and we will take it from there.

Patrick Keating,
Keating & Associates, Inc, An Independent Firm
Raymond James Financial Services, Inc.
Securities offered through Raymond James Financial Services, Inc. Member FINRA/SIPC